AT ALL EXPENDS

In Verse

Rick Bryan

Copyright © 2022 by Rick Bryan
All rights reserved

CONTENTS

An Instance Set
As The Considered
At All Expends
In Reading
In Sentiment
Infinitive
It Gets
It Would Were
Out Of The Picturesque
Part Of That
Some Paused Gesture
The Hour As
The Informal Of
The Water
The Words Will
There Which
To The Issue Tresse
Turned
Under And Around
Well Of The Quill

At All Expends

In
Verse

AN INSTANCE SET

An instance set such to speak
To mention to which a semblance
A placing of garland
And discontinuous
In part intervals the last
The order of factor be granted
Is the hint contrived

Drawn back an impetus
Surface of water to a point
Circulars of open air for which
Contrasts audacity dispense
In the idea of incident
Intermingles the whistling row

Outlined as the eye aspected
Surrounding of facet
Did not constrain in overlay
By a throw assumption under
The premise at all regard
Which reveals momentus late
A point takes observed.

Soundscape: Light In My Head /
Mr. Cloudy

AS THE CONSIDERED

As the considered as
The onset and bid of you
All the well anything like
Still sooner of it shone
For the day in form of

In the late crown over
A denude of all
No doubt a petty aside

And drawn in a verge
Flight as the fisher bound
A short hand entrust
In a word what assuming
So you say to that at all.

Soundscape: Water's Edge /
Gerald Clayton

AT ALL EXPENDS

At all expends the most
Upheaval entails at length
Perhaps per soon the underline
Of earth the swing you would push

First of the scripting point
Of various written
Terms regress under
Emerge the manner current
And other by to the like
A threshold for

For that in a year's trace
The timbre of sound it is
On to the roof of hope of
This way standing there or
Even quite to the drafting of
Flowers denoting in full.

Soundscape: This Time / Matthew Halsall

IN READING

In reading fraught of water

The overwhelm the flotsam and spell
Lay it was precipitate lost for it
Silver me all rush over swept
What troubled in waters an aside
More so was a course at which
Cast was helm beyond ranged a
Would have a gamble good humble
Far sighted to swells out from what
At all leeway first sail there risen

In course shellback over scrawled
Gone chance to consider high tidal
The intact and fallow or might to the
Fairing grasped may assume thus
Oceanus a plume nautical by tens
Irrevocable off up went the night
Water profusion the risen over
Embayed the matter reasoned by
Even though either so farewell first sea

Soundscape: Orange Nights / Jens Buchert

As has a turned such kind the expect
In such way that dialects as for not
That I ask suitable consideration so
For the moment unto the intended and
Promise white buckets awashed in the
Name of coursed the question going a
Rough driving utterly in the name as of
Fares off went were out on a felled
Halyard on seas first port batten.

IN SENTIMENT

In sentiment as you glance
End of in over upon over
In a sense spiraling fragments
Aground and so inlets back to you
An appeal are we to this
As profiles a strictness of sense
Tactful as stepping out
Of the turn and care at all

Undone would all the sky
Of nothing to impending of
The matter and in and under
For bearing out you take
Of a crowd so as not half heard
Various as for reminisce lines of seam
Days await on the platform per chance
In edge slants of you.

Soundscape: Together / Matthew Halsall

INFINITIVE

Infinitive an air
A slight pictured as
Inclined inclined to
Aspirance of water

Neither collage nor
Scatter of masquerade
Pedestaled stylus
Over bright luminous

As the might have
Beginning over end
Of interior placed
December in aspect.

Soundscape: Early Autumn / George Shearing

IT GETS

It gets onto the latter by which
A bit more up to then
In which are and the gap and
Other a core of the term use
As three two one equates
Or so as would you see it

Was that the mere
An out looking much
A placed pin a number of
And to rather than of
A second tier turned through
Tended press other you tell

Much a sense a going back
The rather cut tip one way a turn
Itself in order of the soil and
That played out in third onsets
A closer look reflecting
That of which you refrain.

Soundscape: Arc / Ishq

IT WOULD WERE

It would were that it would
In the appearance of image of
The long noon's hot and quiet
In the shone and whence
Footfall there'd be and slant
Beyond long livid here where
And wall and side a touch of

All the wide air about
As may seem so as
Down folded hands and
Here centers the sheer point
Straight line of town and place
Lamps mist and mire
As you've along the furrow
One suspects abstractus.

Soundscape: Forest Dub / Runo

OUT OF THE PICTURESQUE

Out of the picturesque has the
Down beheld upon the hazel
Gold so to whether or
Embroidery and silent of
Her hand upon in blue kerchief
As the surface a fountain
In wake the deep and the
And statuesque form and close

The as would notioned of
Listens the murmur to the catch
At midlight a vague rose of hour
Far end and set a threshold well of it
In the swift at all you get on to
It overcasts to what is
Recalled and subdued else listless
And languid the rain on oneself
Falling of lilacs as may

Soundscape: Dorsem / Aaron Diehl Trio

Of morning luxuriant on the breach
That to an instance
Lapse aught it doesn't matter
A bit sulky like yet to notice
To the presence of theory some time will
You have the final by and not
Of there as somehow time of your life
The winding fancy and clamor
And remembered in the dusk
Voices the gaze into light.

PART OF THAT

*Part of that
Fade over assumption
In the cities now ever appear
And which one reason for the widening
In the blue it becomes in the shift
A gap at all a rouge in the yield
Does the good for to the to clear seen*

*Hard reading a loosening
Under which likely all shown
Gotten of was going on
Looking the means as given
Single strands out entail
Enfract a some sort the cover like
Played out in onset a closer most likely*

*Slip a turnaround rebounds
And dusts again similarly of and
In a way the peg storms
Reason of change is it so
Patients me of this quite apart of
Drifting on and off at issue
That of memorandum.*

Soundscape: Slow Dancing In the Dark / Joji

SOME PAUSED GESTURE

Some paused gesture as for
Into the deep the blue press and flow
There a star sigh and over the catch
Outwash and abide to sun pale there
Stands one after one of a hundred things
High windless the smoke blushes of
Water after rain and hush and flowers
Yet your feet tread painted aflame
The morning arise and through the sleep

Dew and noon in the hover the wind of
To wing to breath to the white shear sea
And earth shaken of the whirling shoal
Keep and will up to the and turn away
Neither without nor hill and crest
As here slips that seeks breathless

Soundscape: Stillpoint / Purl

Eyes to over sake thought and shape
Swift pearled the green above taken by
Unflailing clear of time the height
Evening one in the gold horn of light
Or known idle and perplex the while
And greater things and recall still so
Lightly as the skies by hour for which
Today all this day that being.

THE HOUR AS

The hour as to and so
Else well of
The vast aspected
En route
In the manner galley of

What would have trowel in hand
And would have
As implication by such
Of a puzzle into place or guise
In the day ready piece

In which
Wouldn't have of it
And furthering specious
Evasive in corridors

Dear of radiant
Else the air as well
In maginot threading
Daybreak envelopes.

Soundscape: This Time / Matthew Halsall

THE INFORMAL OF

The informal of sound
Or gathering part word such
Rather as rendered such
Upon my heart of a certain

Dismissive after term is the pitch
Infidius livid by sum number of
On into the jot something to
Now well the circle of

Anxious is the aim hit
A holding it is to consider
And of this to play in scale
In which they would have

Derivative notes the light of
Fields of octave as were
Filled deep to the down
Invocation the haze about

Soundscape: Together (Special Edition) /
Matthew Halsall

*That to me interval spanned
Precursor these lengths of time
Affectidely a fair side of
Quite highly the air ceremonious.*

THE WATER

The water glittered in the sun
It goes well my pleasure

A mingling up than when which
Something in relation to breakwater
At length about drawn as
Sands in heaviness immense
Or of down to its catch brings

Other sake may that you are
Ideas for a way suggests
Does so in tone a place and
Principle such as cycles in
Crossings of opposites the flux

Order of lament shades outwardly
Addresses entire fuse the
Distance between somewhat by irony
Contrary an expressive prevailing
In much so fledged first of

Soundscape: Notre Dame de Paris - Garou - Belle (Live)

*Courses a light of matters and veiled
Other would have of becoming
Much to do indelible far more
Into thin air questionnaires and
In waters' redress so on.*

THE WORDS WILL

The words will get me
Nowhere to find out
Leaves abaundant sparse
Of granite tree stump or post
A sail mast rooted stalk
The sea deep water on
The line on the mooring
In depth of dark clear

Cannot be at all I swear
If it were in doubt that
Somehow in bloom in flower
Beds the river for you
And sleep and sleep glides
And I know dawn was of
Laid away and that
Would have been.

Soundscape: Life On Line / Moarn

THERE WHICH

There which as to of thee
Drawn it becomes of the still
Form of aspect a brash interlude
Carries that then devising
None the less as well formal shapes
Painting as entire not the end of

Flamboyant catch all or other supposed
In gesture than else resolve and whim
Of crowds effect the scuffle what holds
Account subsequent masks in variance

Rendered so set contrivance
Turned to vie for what do you then
As over slight imaged
Etched as such cut the clear that
Upon the while at any rate
Of the reveal accorded.

Soundscape: Dawn Sleepy Dub / Dublicator

TO THE ISSUE TRESSE

To the issue tresse
The clear and the hour
A care what the life of
What as pleases would a difference
Would it matter oh my rose the sum I will
Of it crossed gleam and waver
More such along of appeared
In withheld in swarm jostle revel
Were it seemed the quite of

Oh trivial exchange of time of manner
And remains such as remembrance
Overwhelm fraught and spell lay
It was as correspondent for the
Vague of entity altogether of course
Only just in just now on the other hand
None such of knowing the winding
One would a word to me now
For I'd regard essentially now
Having read as of a few lines
Looking upon considering drawn

*Soundscape: Naps in Costa Rica /
Sweatson Klank*

Of the well the rivulet beneath flowed it
Fell on the green moss as were
The flame aflail well by well
And the tangle in the winds burning of
Dream of air faint upon rain
Round and round the sun as overlain
What it looks on the beheld amethyst
Be it so grass among as I passed
Away and turned with all where I stood

Above of earth ever sea as given
Wings by weave into the slade
Forth crossed the broad a glance
Beneath wide and the sea the slip sails
On and on the ridge the slant
Clouds in the distance of the lifelong
Where that bells the rails a day
In the balance hour form
In a month of though in current
Of the tide the embank.

TURNED

Turned of aspect the draw line
Of at all the other sums of color
On canvas even now when
At all with all back to you ago
Your hair and hands best I knew
And account one would well and

So it does reason which darts
In volume of key the hour fragment
Still one would though slight
This or that the order woven and
Movement and heard there changing
Winds and gesture and you only

This and here of in pulse of mind
Back thoughts given sights and
Sound and gleaming dust the light
Cast close and bright by way
Sheen each in each into the
Firelight form of arc.

Soundscape: G.R.I.T. - Closure /
Harrison Divecha

UNDER AND AROUND

Under and around background
Mirrored in turning to speak aside
Across the view I mean by
All that indirects as for

Open vanished sky white clouds
East west the moment or other
Ready set all bearing in mind
As away far enough

A part of or place just
Unrolls is the sheen was considered
Easily is the wind of a course
No matter it subjects streaked so

Or in other instance of
Down sets and to one or other
Facades the eye of light and
Obscurity the edge seams
As of and here to as well.

Soundscape: Blue And Green / Renzo Ruggieri

WELL OF THE QUILL

Well of the quill and oblique
It was not of a certain
The general air invocation
Enough the ambiguities of surface
Sensitivity is the year held
Sense of lightness of circumstance
In the manner of vast aspected

Well of the hour as so
And would have would have
Specious in the day or guise
Evasive in corridor and furthering
The air as well dear of radiant
Maginot threading else
Aquatine daybreaks envelopes in.

Soundscape: Treefingers / Radiohead

Made in the USA
Middletown, DE
27 October 2022

13636447R00022